Otaku and K-pop: The Fusion of Fan Cultures

 In the realm of global fandoms, two distinct subcultures have captured the hearts of millions: otaku and K-pop.

 Otaku culture, originating from Japan, celebrates the love for anime, manga, and related media.

  Meanwhile, K-pop, a music genre from South Korea, has taken the world by storm with its infectious melodies and captivating performances.

This book explores the intersection of these fan cultures, highlighting the shared passion, cross-pollination of interests, and the harmonious relationship that exists between otaku and K-pop enthusiasts.

Understanding Otaku Culture

Otaku culture revolves around a deep passion for Japanese anime, manga, and other forms of pop culture.

 Otaku enthusiasts immerse themselves in captivating storylines, unique art styles, and the imaginative worlds depicted in anime and manga.

From the sprawling epic sagas to slice-of-life narratives and fantastical adventures, otaku find solace, inspiration, and a sense of belonging within these mediums.

The otaku community thrives on conventions, online forums, and social media platforms where fans can connect, share recommendations, and express their creativity through cosplay, fan art, and fanfiction.

The Rise of K-pop

K-pop, short for Korean pop music, has experienced an explosive rise in popularity over the past decade.

Characterized by catchy melodies, synchronized choreography, and stunning visuals, K-pop has captivated fans around the world.

The genre's success can be attributed to its talented artists, meticulous production values, and the strong connection K-pop agencies forge with fans through social media platforms.

K-pop fandoms, known as "stans," have become a force to be reckoned with, demonstrating incredible loyalty and support for their favorite idols.

The Overlapping Appeal

While otaku and K-pop culture may seem distinct at first glance, they share common threads that make them complementary fan cultures.

Many K-pop music videos feature vibrant visuals inspired by anime and manga, incorporating elements such as magical powers, fantastical settings, and intricate storytelling.

K-pop groups often create concept albums and music videos that resonate with otaku fans, drawing them into a captivating world that aligns with their interests and passions.

Cosplay and Fan Art: A Harmonious Blend

Cosplay, a significant aspect of otaku culture, has found its place in the world of K-pop fandom.

Many K-pop enthusiasts enjoy creating costumes inspired by their favorite idols and performances, showcasing their dedication and creativity at conventions and fan events.

Similarly, fan art has become a bridge between otaku and K-pop fandoms, as talented artists create stunning illustrations merging elements of anime, manga, and K-pop idols.

This convergence of creative expressions strengthens the bond between otaku and K-pop enthusiasts and fosters a sense of shared admiration for visual arts.

Global Collaborations and Cultural Exchange

The influence of otaku and K-pop culture is not limited to their respective countries of origin.

K-pop music videos often reference Japanese pop culture, incorporating anime-inspired visuals, fashion styles, and iconic references that resonate with otaku fans.

Likewise, Japanese anime series have utilized K-pop music as opening and ending themes, introducing K-pop to a broader audience and sparking interest in the genre.

The cross-pollination of these fan cultures through collaborations, music crossovers, and joint events has created a symbiotic relationship that amplifies the reach and impact of both otaku and K-pop cultures on a global scale.

   Otaku and K-pop represent two vibrant and passionate fan cultures that have captivated millions worldwide.

   Their shared love for creative storytelling, captivating visuals, and immersive worlds has fostered a natural connection between otaku and K-pop enthusiasts.

Through the blending of anime-inspired visuals, cosplay, fan art, and cultural exchanges, these fan cultures continue to inspire and entertain fans across borders. The fusion of otaku and K-pop culture showcases the power of fandom, transcending language and cultural barriers, and uniting individuals through a shared appreciation for artistic expression and the joy of being part of a supportive community.

Thank you for reading. We've included space below for your notes also.